The First 30 Days in
Heaven

Amy Quonce

The First 30 Days in Heaven
Copyright © Amy Quonce 2014

ISBN-13: 978-0989090414
ISBN-10:0989090418

For Dan, who taught me everything I know about true love.

He looked like he was sleeping; snuggled tightly in bed with his head gracefully resting on the pillow. It wasn't until I went to touch him did I realized he had drifted off into an eternal rest.

The phone call to emergency services was easier than the ones I had to make to family and friends. They were right there by his side though ...every one of them. We took turns saying goodbye and finding comfort in one another's arms. No matter how much I pleaded, his eyes remained closed.

Nobody was prepared for him to leave. He was too young and had so much still to do on this earth. I was far too young to be left alone and labeled a widow. It wasn't fair to anybody.

When the chaos settled down many hours later, I prayed. Prayed that he went in peace, and that he was in a better place. I Prayed he would forgive me if I ever made him feel unloved. Prayed that my husband would always watch over me from above.

Then I prayed some more. I prayed I would wake up in the morning and learn this had all been a bad dream.

"Mommy, why did my Daddy have to die?"

I woke up this morning. My first thought: my husband still didn't. He'll never have the luxury of waking up to the sunshine again.

Everyone is gone and the house is eerily quiet. My body remains numb from last night's events, so at the moment I don't feel a thing. Is that normal?

Once out of bed, I pace the house trying to figure out what to do. After several laps I realized unless I tried to keep a normal routine, I would drive myself nuts.

After my shower I scooped up the dog and bring him to the groomers. His appointment had been set up weeks ago and I figured if he was there for the day, at least it would be one less thing I would have to worry about. I kept a stoic face as I handed him over and walked back to my car. Now it is just me and my thoughts to fill the day.

My mind keeps replaying the events from the night before. They didn't seem real. My body gently rocks back and forth in an effort to calm my reality. My husband is gone.

When I pull back into my driveway I see family is waiting there. They look at me with disbelief in their eyes and hug me until I hurt. They sit with me and together we share stories of my husband over the food they brought.

As evening approaches, more and more people reach out to me for comfort. Each one offering to help in any way they can.

Can any of them bring my husband back? Right now, that's all that I need.

Plans need to be made. There are flowers to pick out, new clothes to buy, people to notify, an announcement to write for the paper, and a place for the service needs to be decided.

We made very similar decisions when we planned our wedding...except it's nothing like that now. Instead of happiness, these arrangements are being done in sorrow.

What about the plans we already made?

There were places we wanted to visit, things we were going to do, and a future that was already spoken for. We've been making these plans for years.

How am I supposed to decide on final matters in just a few days?

We vaguely talked about his last wishes. The one thing he was adamant on was the t-shirt he was to wear under his suit. He mentioned it several times, yet I never embedded it into my brain. I figured when his time came that shirt would have been long ago discarded with tattered holes and stains. Now, I frantically search and search to find the one I think he was talking about. Please, don't let me get the one thing he asked for wrong.

The rest of the details I'm sure he couldn't care less about. During our marriage he was only concerned with choosing the right flower arrangements for me. He never worried about where an event was being held, as long as we were together. Even though I chose a nice urn instead of a simple coffee can for his remains, I'm sure he'd be okay with the decision.

All the preparations that are made for a funeral are really for those left behind. We want to make sure we give our loved ones a proper send off, and offer one last final gesture of love to them.

They are only concerned we loved them to begin with. Love is all that truly matters.

The funeral director asks me to bring down the clothes I wish to lay my husband to rest in.

I scramble through his dresser praying his favorite t-shirt wasn't in the dirty clothes basket, so I could honor his wish. Thankfully, I find it in the bottom drawer. With that out of the way, I go to the closet and take out his suit he had bought for himself one New Years Eve night and had surprised me with a night out on the town. I unzip the bag and hang his t-shirt on the hanger underneath the dress shirt, and then find clean under garments and socks to place in the bag as well. The only thing left was his dress shoes.

Darn it, where did I see them last? I had cleaned out the closet a few weeks prior, but for the life of me I cannot remember where I moved the shoes to. I frantically search the bedroom, and when I can't find them I throw myself on the bed crying uncontrollably. This was to be the last thing I could do for my husband, and I was failing because I couldn't find him shoes to wear.

After an hour, I lift my head off the pillow and start to search again. My inner voice speaks up and tells me to look under the bed. Lifting the dust ruffle, I see the shoe box sitting there. I slide it out, lift the lid, and stare at the shoes that had only been worn a handful of times. They still had a shine to them. I put the cover back on and place it in the suit bag with the rest of his clothes.

My husband would be properly dressed, but what about me? I didn't own anything suitable for his funeral. Taking a long deep breath, I head out to the mall. Usually I love visiting the mall, but this time I was trying to shop with tears in my eyes. I head toward the dresses and look through all the styles that offered black as a color option. Taking a few off the rack, I go to the dressing room to try them on.

It is imperative I get a style my husband would approve of. Even in his death, I want to impress him. One by one, I try on the array of classy styled dresses.

Looking in the mirror, I try to imagine his response to each. He used to love watching me get dressed each morning, telling me I looked beautiful no matter what I wore. Still, I can't decide.

I ignore the sales lady who asks if I was shopping for anything special and offered to assist me. There just isn't a polite response to "I'm shopping for my husband's funeral so please leave me alone because this is hard enough as it is."

After I settle on a sleek respectable looking dress, I pick out a fresh pair of tights and new shoes. I now owned an outfit I never wanted to wear, and certainly would never wear again.

My husband is in the paper today.

Right there, under the obituaries, is the article I wrote for him. His smiling face stared back at me as I paid for the newspaper and rush out of the store. The picture was from one of our first vacations together. When I took it, I never imagined it would be used for a final goodbye.

The story talked about what a great man he was. How he loved to watch Nascar, and enjoyed campfires with the family on warm summer nights. I wonder if he got to do everything he wanted in life. Was there something that would have made him feel complete that I could have added to his obituary? I guess I'll never know.

When I get home, I clip the section out and gingerly carry it to the bedroom. As I sit on the bed, I read it over and over. It's right there in black and white, so how can I deny it any longer? He is never coming back.

It's too painful to look at, so I tuck it away in a memory box. A memory I wish I could erase.

I dress alone in the morning. Piece by piece, I put on those clothes I had been dreading, and then leave to get my hair done. I didn't care if it sounded silly. My husband loved the way I looked every time I came home from the hairdresser. Since this was to be the last time our physical bodies would be together, I want to look my best for him.

I enter the salon looking the part of a grieving wife, trying to hide my tears behind dark sunglasses. Conversation was to a minimum, yet the tension was high. Everyone knew why I was there, yet no one knew the right words to say. When my hair was done, I drive home and wait to be escorted to the funeral home.

Behind the sadness was a small glimmer of eagerness. I needed to see my husband again. It had been several days and today finally I was getting the chance to put my eyes on him. My heart knew he wouldn't look the same as the last time I saw him, but I still longed to be near his body once more.

As the funeral director opens the door for me to enter the room where his coffin is, I nearly run to his side. My fingers tousle his hair, and then I slid my hand in with his. I stare at him for the longest time, trying to capture every feature he had in my mind. Then, I lay my head on his chest and cry. When the tears ran out, I take the opportunity to tell him everything I never had a chance to tell him before. I apologize for trivial things, and make promises to him for the future. I breathe him in and brace myself for the realization that this would be our last time together. I wasn't ready to share this moment with anyone else, yet I knew in a few minutes, hundreds of people would be there to say goodbye to him as well.

When friends and family start arriving, my body shifts into robot-mode. Shake hands, give hugs, and repeat what a tragedy this was. Hour after hour, I function on auto-pilot. Soon, the funeral director brings out chairs in preparation for the sermon to start. I sit next to my best friend, grab her hand, and never let go.

The preacher's words drift in and out of my ears as my eyes are fixed on my husband lying on display in front of me. He looks so peaceful, so handsome. When the service concludes, I walked toward the coffin and throw myself onto my husband. I don't want this to end.

Once the coffin is closed, I will never
lay eyes on him again.

**"Mommy, which cloud is Daddy
watching us from today?**

As hunger finally starts to creep in for the first time in days, I look through the kitchen to find something to eat. The food people brought over had long since been gone, and the only edible items left in the house are "his food." Everyone has food only a certain person in the house will eat, and now his was staring at me, screaming out that he will never be back to eat them.

Their presence haunts me. I know if I don't act now, I would never be able to go through with it. One by one, I put the food in the trash, pausing long enough in between items to reminisce about a time when he had enjoyed them. When the house was completely emptied, I leave for the store.

There has never been a time when vegetables have made me so sad. He had always wanted a variety of different vegetables at each meal, and I always bought them just for him. Now, I walk by them with a tear in my eye. I won't be needing hot peppers again, and the thought of that is more than I can handle.

Each aisle aroused a different memory for me; of us cooking together, eating meals as a family, and both agreeing what a horrible chef I am. Food used to serve as a reason for us to spend quality time with one another. It will never be the same for me again, and I think I may shed a tear each time I see his favorite dish.

I turn on the radio to drown out the thoughts in my head. I just need a few moments to try to absorb everything. As soon as I push the button on, our song starts to play.

I close my eyes and am instantly transported back a few weeks when he had his arms wrapped around my waist, dancing with me in the kitchen to that very tune. We side- stepped in a circle as the music played, nuzzling each other's noses every so often. I could still feel it as if it was really happening, and I dance alone in the kitchen as if it were.

The feeling is so strong, I never want to forget it. I rush to my computer and search for any other songs that would spark a memory of us. One after another, I download a collection of music representing our entire lives. Music really does speak to the heart.

Now, I only need the rhythm of certain tunes to bring me back to him. They go with me in the car, on long walks, and are by my side during lonely nights. When I hear them, he is still alive within me. Some say that music can heal the soul. I sure hope they're right.

"Mommy, what planet is Heaven on?"

It's 3:00 am, and I find myself wandering aimlessly through the house. Sleep eludes me anyway, and looking at his things makes me feel closer to him. I try on his glasses, smell his pencils, and rub the soft fabric of his favorite blanket between my fingers. I temporarily allow myself to become him.

What was he thinking those last few moments of life? Did he know the last time he used those pliers was going to be his last? There are so many questions, and so few answers.

The house is quiet as I explore his world. It's always quiet now. I don't like it. What I would give to be able to ask him to turn down the television one more time because it was too loud. To be able to argue with him over trivial thing, then hear the beautiful "I'm sorry, I really do love you" words upon our making up. To be woken up in the morning by the sound of a saw buzzing as he worked in the garage. I miss those sounds.

I miss him.

Has the bed always been this big?

I still curl up on the right side of the mattress, just as I had when he was still here. Only now, it seems like the empty space between me and his side goes on forever. In the middle of the night, I reach over to touch him. My empty hand reminds me that I will never be able to touch him again.

I no longer have to fight for blankets or listen to his snoring at night. I can keep the temperature as warm as I like while I sleep. Did I really used to complain over such trivial things?

The bed now looks perfectly made when I get up in the morning because all I did was lie awake all night. His favorite quilt quietly covers up his spot, but it cannot blanket the truth. He has passed into a place where he no longer needs physical comfort and warmth.

But I still need them. I still need him.

"Mommy, what is Daddy's new phone number in Heaven?"

As hard as it was to grocery shop for the
first time since my husband went to live in
Heaven, doing the laundry is even harder.
My house has long since been neglected,
and I need something to occupy my mind. I
find the over-flowing basket of clothes and
head to the laundry room.

Absentmindedly, I dump the basket into
the wash and walk away to clean other areas
of the house. The clothes pass from the
washer to dryer between my dusting, but
when the dryer cycle ends, it hist me like a
ton of bricks.

The freshly warm fabrics of my
husband's clothes were ready to be put
away...and never to be taken out again. This

will be the last time I would wash his favorite race car shirt, and the new jeans I had given him for Christmas. His holey socks that never got mended should be thrown away, but how could I discard his clothes like that? I can't.

I pick up a few more pieces and snuggle my face into them, breathing in his scent. I can still smell him, despite the clothes being freshly washed. I love his smell.

Tears fall down, soiling the clothes I had just cleaned, but I don't wipe them away. Neatly, I fold each piece and place them back in the drawer where my husband had last taken them out, and then close it tight.

Staring at the walls in the house is getting redundant. I think I'll go to the store and wander around aimlessly looking at their walls. Maybe a change of scenery will do me some good.

Part of me thinks it feels good to get out of the house; the other part is second-guessing my decision. I wander through the aisles looking at nothing in particular when I notice some familiar faces. Thankfully, they don't see me, so I quickly change my direction to avoid them like the plague. Instantly I feel guilty, but I'm just not up for receiving any more hugs or having to relive the whole story of how my husband passed again.

I'm able to get through two more aisles before my luck runs out. Somebody rushes toward me with the saddest look on their face. I'm quickly swept into their arms and am forced to listen to what a great guy my husband was. I already knew he was a great guy. Why can't this person let me continue my charade that he's just at work right now? Can't they talk about him as if he were still here?

As much as I don't want to hear it, I really do appreciate people trying to console me. All their kind words will eventually help me ease into reality. Plus, the stories the share with me will become part of my memories as well, and one can never have too many wonderful memories of their loved ones.

I called his phone today.

One part of my brain is telling me I am crazy, that nobody is going to answer. The other part tells me to never give up hope. I let it ring over and over. When the voicemail comes on, I hang up and dial it again.

After I am disappointed, I go to my computer's inbox. I bring up every email he ever sent me and hit the print button. Page after page of simply precious words came pouring out of the machine.

He signed every letter with X's and O's beneath his name. Not just one or two of them, but a whole strand, and in bold capital letters. He was never shy about expressing his love.

My husband was a great man like that.

The flowers are wilted.

All that remains from the once-vibrant bouquets at his funeral are dry leaves, droopy buds, and petals falling on the floor at an alarming rate. They are also starting to stink. I know I need to get rid of them, but that is easier said than done. Once they are gone, so is the symbol for what they stood for-the love all his family and friends shared with him in his final moment.

I try for a few hours to work the courage up to empty the vases, but the emotional strength just isn't there. In sheer desperation, I call my family to come over to do it for me. I just can't be the one to erase them from existence.

Luckily, my family has a better idea. Instead of throwing the flowers away, I can peel off each wilting petal, allow them to dry out completely, and turn them into potpourri. For the first time since my husband's death, I was enthusiastic. I now had a way to preserve their memory and make use of them. For the next four hours, I peel back thousands of flower petals, and intrinsically place them on baking sheets to dry out. By the time I am done, the floor of my laundry room had been transformed into a beautiful array of colors.

Bare stems was now all that stood between me and my first step of moving forward. I bundle them up in my arms, walk into the backyard, and scattered the stems as if I were spreading his ashes. They were now free to rejoin the earth and energize the soil for more things to grow.

The empty vases and baskets that once held beautiful arrangements will now be used to cradle the potpourri. I leave the ribbons intact and carefully begin to place the baskets around the house where I can permanently display them.

There were two displays, however, which are extra special to me; the one I had bought for his funeral, and the arrangement he had sent to me at work the day before he passed. I find the picture I had taken of them both, and take it to the craft store. There, I buy fabric flowers to recreate the bouquets and place those gently on the shelf in my bedroom next to his urn.

Two beautiful bouquets now bloom in honor of one beautiful human being.

It's the middle of the night and I'm crying again.

During the day I can manage to contain my composure, but when it's dark out, I am free to let the tears loose.

While I curl up into a ball, I feel the bed decompress and a soft pressure snuggles up against my lower back. I smile. Man's best friend. I can always count on him to be there in my time of need. It's comforting to have someone near. The tears flow fast as I lay still, feeling the warmth of my pet beside me.

Eventually, I turn over to pet the dog, but he's not there. I get up and search the house only to find him fast asleep in my daughter's arms. He was never in my room. Could it be possible I experienced a visit and felt my husband's soul climb into bed and comfort me while I cried over him?

That would be just like him to go to the ends of the earth to console me in my time of need.

"Mommy, how will Daddy be able to come back to Earth and visit us?

I am one who likes to plaster.

Often when a loved one passes, those left behind will do one of two things; either they hide all the photos of the dearly departed, or plaster them excessively around the house trying to remember every little detail. I fall into the second category.

My house always had pictures of my husband on display, but now that he was gone, it isn't enough for me. I need to be able to see him no matter where in the house I am.

That's how the shrine began.

I spend hours combing through photographs and ordering enlargements of certain prints. I create a photo book of his life, and then another of our lives together. Each one gets meticulously displayed to pay homage to a great man.

My house now looks like a crazy woman lives here.

Maybe someday I will be able to take them down, but for now, I need these pictures. I need to look at them when I talk to him, and I need to hold them against me to try and recapture an embrace. It's not the same kissing a glass frame, but it's all I have left, and I will kiss it each and every day.

It's 6:00. I look out the window expecting my husband to pull into the driveway. He always comes home from work at this time. Why isn't he here yet?

I guess my mind has gotten the best of me. It's so easy to think nothing has changed, even though everything has changed. I suppose I may always look for him to come home after work, ready to greet me with a huge kiss. That's how it's always been and I'm not ready for it to end.

How will I ever manage to make it through birthdays or holidays if I'm still waiting for him to walk through the front door? Will I ever be able to eat dinner and not notice that there is an empty spot where he always sat?

I think I'll stare out the window some more, just in case I catch a glimpse of him.

My husband's car smells like a concoction
of fast food and tools. It's the first time I've
been in here since he passed. His hat is still
in the backseat where he tossed it and a half-
empty soda bottle awaits to be finished in
the front console.

I can still remember the last time we
were in here together. Holding hands and
singing along to songs blaring from the
speakers. How I wish we could do that
again. I turn on the radio to bring me back in
time.

Looking around, he certainly wasn't the
neatest person, but right now I treasure the
trash around me. Reading the discarded
receipts is like reliving the moments he

spent. I bet he never thought that he'd be leaving me behind a small piece of his life when he tossed them down there.

Ever so gently, I caress the photos he kept in the front seat. They were always with him wherever he went, and now their memory is all I have left to keep him with me. As I sift through the pile, I come across a hidden treasure. Two signed holiday cards from him; one for me and one for our daughter. He had them hidden so they would be a surprise for us when Easter came.

Giving my daughter a card from her daddy after he had passed away was bitter-sweet.

"Mommy, why is Daddy making it rain on us?"

Pennies from Heaven. A phrase I always assumed was mythical until it happened to me.

Filling out legal paperwork left me sad and distraught. At one point I whisper to myself, "*How am I going to carry on alone?*" That's when it happened. Sitting atop of the papers I had been filling out for over 15 minutes, appears a shiny penny.

How it got there cannot be logically explained, but after I found it, a feeling of calmness comes over me. I take it as a sign from my dear husband to let me know he will always be with me, even in spirit.

Several more times shiny pennies suddenly appeared in front of me. A single cent each time to represent all the sense our marriage made. I proudly display them in a heart shaped pattern next to my husband's urn.

Our love refuses to waiver, even through different dimensions.

Find a penny, pick it up, and all that day you'll have good luck.

My husband's eye doctor called today. They wanted to remind him of an upcoming appointment. I have to tell them he wouldn't need this appointment, or any other appointment ever again. The receptionist's once-chipper voice sounds suddenly somber as she apologizes. My hands tremble as I hang up the phone.

Opening the mail isn't any easier. So many things still come in his name. Oh, how I love to see his name on things. It makes it seem like he's here. Even if it's junk mail, I can't bring myself to throw it away. How many more times will I get the opportunity to receive something of his? Deep down I know it will eventually fade away, so I start a pile for everything that comes in, and now and then I sift through it.

Maybe it's easy for businesses to hit the delete button and erase my husband's name from their database, but my mind doesn't work that way. He will never be forgotten or replaced. He was once here, and touched many lives. Something that special can never be erased.

"Mommy, the house is so quiet without Daddy here."

I love my best friend. Every time she comes over to the house she makes a point to visit my husband's urn and talk to him. It's never just a quick awkward hello, but an actual conversation. She'll tell him how much I miss him, what's going on in my life, and how she's watching after me. I need to hear that.

Every morning I kiss my husband hello. His picture is sitting next to my bed, and I place the photo of his lips against mine and kiss him tenderly. I'll talk to him as if he were sitting next to me. He'll hear all about my day at work and what errands I have to run. I still ask his opinion on my choice of outfits (this time it's a plus because I can always pretend he thinks I look fantastic no matter what I choose to wear!)

Yes, sometimes I even yell at him. I curse at him because he left me alone to deal with a broken hot water tank, and because now I'm the one who is stuck taking out the trash now. These were supposed to be his jobs. Then I hold his picture tight to my chest and forgive him for leaving me alone. It wasn't his choice to go, so I shouldn't hold him responsible.

When I hear my friend talking to my husband, it reassures me that I am not insane for having conversations with him too. It's perfectly natural to want to stay connected to my husband and to know his soul can still hear me.

I only wish I could hear him back.

His body wash still sits in the shower. I can't bring myself to take it off the shelf. I like seeing it there next to mine. Sometimes when I'm longing for him, I open the top and breathe in the scent that was once my husband. It brings back so many memories, and creates so many tears.

This was how he smelled before he left for work, and traces of it often still remained when we snuggled up together at night. A single whiff of it can transport me back to those days.

More often than not, I find myself spraying his cologne on the clothes that are still hanging in our closet. I wrap my arms tight around them, my nose inhaling the vapors. It's as if he's actually still in my arms.

There are work boots on my rug and medications still on the dresser. Each one holds a special memory for me. They were a part of him, and he was a part of me. I can't remove them without feeling as though I have removed him from my life.

Maybe at some point I'll be able to separate his things from his memory, but not now. I'm not ready.

This morning I took out the box of letters my husband had written to me throughout the years. He was quite the romantic. Many times I would find a good-night note tucked away under my pillow when I went to bed. "*Think of me in your dreams tonight as I will be dreaming of you.*" Never before had I felt so loved.

I kept everything he ever gave me; every card, every silly doodle. From the beginning I knew they were special.

I read each one with a huge smile on my face because I can vividly remember the times we spent together. Our love was real and could be seen within this stack of papers in front of me. Each word written in those letters was spoken from his heart, and for that I will forever cherish them within mine.

Back then, I giggled at his spelling when one note said "Have a gods night sleep", but now I am the one hoping that he's sleeping tight in God's arms.

Last night he came to me in my dreams.

He didn't speak, but there he was just the same. I reached out to touch his salt and pepper hair, but my arms wouldn't stretch far enough to reach him.

When I awoke, I sank into a deep depression. Why couldn't my subconscious allow me the luxury of reconnecting with my husband again? His visit was both a treasure and a tease, and I don't know if the chance of another one will ever come again.

I close my eyes and try to will myself back to sleep. Maybe I can re-enter the dream where I left off or at least try to relive the moment. I don't want to forget a single second of this wonder gift.

The miles may be far between here and there
But it's my dream vacation, so I don't care
I'll soar through the skies into the clouds of
white
Anxious to arrive, be it day or night

I hear the weather is beautiful there
And the folks are all real friendly
The scenery is beautiful
With landscapes aplenty

You'll meet me at the front gate
As soon as I arrive
And show me all around
Like my own personal guide

Together we'll explore this breathtaking place
Happy to be in one another's embrace
Music softly plays off in the background
Feelings of love are strong and surround

We'll catch up and reminisce
Of all those years ago
And promise to make more memories
And never let them go

But as everything does
My time here will end
I'll need to go back home
And miss you once again

I'll never be able to truly visit here, it seems
For this place is found only in my dreams
It's when I close my eyes and wish for fate
That there could be visiting hours at Heaven's
gate

Dear Dan,

My car is broke and the outside faucet is spraying water everywhere.

You've only been gone a few short weeks; I haven't had time to ease into the role of Mrs. Fix-It. I could always count on you to fix these things without any worries on my part. Now it's up to me to figure out how I'm going to get them repaired.

Why does everything happen at once? I wish the world would cut me some slack and finally allow things to go my way. My mind is still so foggy I can't think clearly, and these are important matters. Why didn't I let you teach me how to fix things around the home?

I had plenty of opportunities to watch you at work, yet never asked you to show me how. I guess I thought I'd never need to know. You were always going to be there to take care of things.

Maybe you heard me shout up to the sky asking for your help, because suddenly I remembered the name of a repair man you spoke about once. Maybe he'll let me observe what he's doing so next time I might be able to do it myself.

Just like everything else I have to do since you left. I don't like it.

Love,
Your wife

Today I laughed.

I didn't mean to, but there I was mindlessly watching television when it happened. I feel guilty. I shouldn't be laughing. My whole life was just turned upside down. What's wrong with me?

I tell my grief counselor about it. She says it's ok to laugh. It's our minds way of telling us it needs a break from all the heavy turmoil. My brain must be on to something because I feel as though I'm heading towards a nervous breakdown.

Later that evening, when the sky was dark and the house grew quiet, I started remembering. I remember all the times we laughed together, and the not so funny times when I wanted to ring his neck. I laugh so hard at one point I forgot what I was laughing about.

I think I'm losing my mind.

When the laughing subsides, I smile. I grin reminiscing about our first date. I giggled at his lame attempts to fold the laundry correctly. Suddenly, I have a thousand reasons to uncurl my face and let my smile shine. We had a good life together, and I am grateful for every minute of it.

It felt good to laugh. I hope I will be able to do it again.

My husband just walked in the store behind me. My mind knows it really can't be him, yet I'm unable to convince my eyes otherwise. I stare in disbelief trying to argue with both my mind and eyes. My heart desperately wants it to be true.

I watch with fixated eyes as this look-a-like glances in my direction, then heads to the meat counter. My heart feels like it will jump out of my chest.

A million scenarios run through my mind. A long awaited reunion between the two of us. A true miracle to be given the chance to reunite with my love. A sad realization that I was offering myself false hope of something that will never be.

I'm shaken so much I have to leave the store. Tears stream down my face faster than I can wipe them off. It has been said that spirit can sometimes show themselves to those who are still grieving. Is it logical? No. But that doesn't mean I didn't wish it were true.

To be given one more chance to say goodbye. To hold your loved one, even for a moment, in your arms again....

"Mommy, when do we get to go to Heaven to live with Daddy again?"

The flower petals are dry!

Now I get to create something beautiful out of a gloomy situation. I get a large bowl and one by one I pick out petals that will complement one another. A red rose petal here, a yellow tulip there. I sprinkle in some baby's breaths and mix them all together. It comes alive with vibrant colors and I add a drop of fragrance to them to enhance the smell.

Gently, I pour the mixture into the first vase that I saved from his funeral and watch as it once again fills up with life. It looks amazing.

Twelve more times I repeat the process until all the dried petals are used up. I get a warm feeling as I sit back and look at them all. Vases big and small contained every type of flower imaginable, swirled together like cornucopia of rainbows.

I neaten up the bows around the outside of the vases and proudly put them back in their place. These flowers will never die. They will no longer represent the grief from his funeral. They have been re-birthed and given the chance to live forever. Just like my husband's soul has.

Despite the pain of losing my husband, there are things about his death I am grateful for.

I am grateful that he passed at home in his sleep. I'm grateful that he went quickly and without terrible suffering. I'm thankful the week prior he had time off from work to relax and spend his last few days doing what he wanted. He was blessed in this aspect.

Not everyone is lucky enough to be able to have such a peaceful ending. I couldn't even begin to imagine how their loved ones can grieve when the passing is complicated by uncontrollable events. No one deserves that kind of pain.

As time passes, I am able to add more things to my list of things I am grateful for.

I am ever so grateful to have had my husband be a part of my life. He has made me a better person. I'm grateful for having the opportunity to discover what true love really means. Every day, I count my blessings for all the gifts he gave me over the years: hugs, kisses, pride, and acceptance. These are irreplaceable.

Yes, even during grief I need to be thankful. For without that, my husband's memory will be in vain.

My Dearest Love,

I can't believe it's been over 30 days since I last saw your face. Every morning I wake up hoping it was all a bad dream, but here I am still alone in this house.

I've missed your gentle kisses each morning and exchanging I love you's at night. What I wouldn't give to lace my fingers inside of yours once again. It was such a blessing to have you be a part of my life. I am thankful for every minute we had together.

I wrote you a story to show you how much you meant to me. I hope you like it: *He had courted me for months, being a true gentleman along the way. Patiently he waited, breaking that sturdy wall down around my heart one piece at a time. It had built up slowly over the years, cemented by*

*the pain I had endured. Where I came from,
I learned not to trust, and that if I let anyone
in, hurt would be my only retribution.*

*Dan didn't seem to mind that I made
him wait three months before I let him kiss
me, or that I replied with a kind thank you
when he expressed his love. It was his
willingness to let me slowly open my heart
that made me fall in love with him in the first
place.*

*Chivalry was second nature to him, yet
all new to me. Where I came from men
didn't respect women. But Dan quickly
changed that. He knew how to treat a lady.
Always opening doors for me and helping
me put on a jacket. Love notes would be
found on my pillow at night and warm
tender kisses touched my lips every morning
before he left for work. He never, ever, went*

a day without telling me how much he loved me. That was my Dan. My sweet loving Dan.

Oh, how he loved sending flowers. For no reason at all I would be surprised by a brightly colored bouquet that smelled just as sweet as the morning sunshine. Often he would take pleasure in handing them to me himself, but every once in a while I would be surprised with a delivery truck dropping off an arrangement. It was just his way to show how much he cared, and that I was special to him.

Of all the flowers I have received over the years, it is the basket of yellow roses with white daises that I will treasure the most. A purple butterfly was perched on the side handle of the basket, and the note attached simply said "Thinking of you, Love Dan."

*These will forever be my favorite as you
sent them to me out of the blue the day
before you went to Heaven.*

*Now I have an angel watching over me
from up above. I may not be able to see him,
but I can still feel his love deep within my
heart. When I close my eyes tight, the vision
of him softly caressing my cheeks with his
fingertips comes rushing back as vividly as
it had when he was still lying by my side.*

*Time may have changed things, but
there is one thing I know for sure now.
Where I come from, there was a kind and
gentle man who showed me the true
meaning of love.*

Life just isn't the same without you,
Dan. How I wish we could have gone to
Heaven together, but the universe had other
plans. I'm not sure why so many people have
to mourn your loss, but maybe in time we

will learn the lesson your passing was suppose to teach us.

We all miss you so much. Being one of those who are left behind, I can see how much of a positive influence you had on this world. You cared for your family, your friends, and for your job. Did you know how much we loved you in return?

If it's not too much to ask, please wait for me by the pearly gates. I want to walk through them together, hand in hand, as if we were starting our lives together once more. I can't promise you how long it will take me to get there, but in the meantime, I will take comfort in knowing that you will help to watch over me until I can reach you.

I love you honey- forever and always.

~Amy

www.ingramcontent.com/pod-product-compliance
Lightning Source LLC
Chambersburg PA
CBHW072014060426
42446CB00043B/2433